Monster Feelings

by Liza Charlesworth

Monster Feelings

by Liza Charlesworth

Illustrated by Steve Mack

www.scholastic.com

ISBN: 978-1-338-18912-6

We Can

by Liza Charlesworth

We Can

by Liza Charlesworth

No part of this publication may be reproduced, stored in a retrieval system, or transmitted in any form or by any means, electronic, mechanical, photocopying, recording, or otherwise, without written permission of the publisher. For information regarding permission, write to Scholastic Inc., Attention: Permissions Department, 557 Broadway, New York, NY 10012.

ISBN: 978-1-338-18913-1
Illustrated by Steve Mack
Art Director: Tannaz Fassihi; Designer: Michelle H. Kim

Copyright © 2017 by Liza Charlesworth. All rights reserved. Published by Scholastic Inc.

10 9 68 21 22 23/0

Printed in China. First printing, June 2017.

www.scholastic.com

ISBN: 978-1-338-18913-1

Cranky Clothes

by Liza Charlesworth

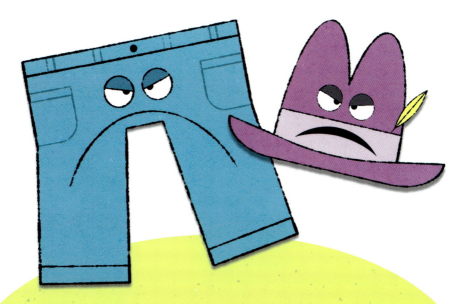

Cranky Clothes

by Liza Charlesworth

No part of this publication may be reproduced, stored in a retrieval system, or transmitted in any form or by any means, electronic, mechanical, photocopying, recording, or otherwise, without written permission of the publisher. For information regarding permission, write to Scholastic Inc., Attention: Permissions Department, 557 Broadway, New York, NY 10012.

ISBN: 978-1-338-18914-8
Illustrated by Steve Mack
Art Director: Tannaz Fassihi; Designer: Michelle H. Kim

Copyright © 2017 by Liza Charlesworth. All rights reserved. Published by Scholastic Inc.

10 9   68   21 22 23/0

Printed in China. First printing, June 2017.

SCHOLASTIC

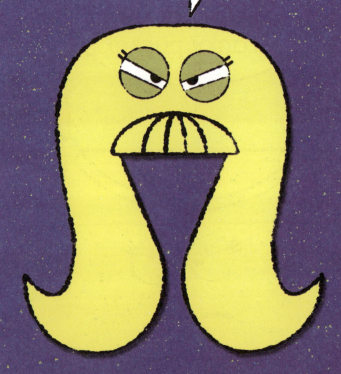

www.scholastic.com

ISBN: 978-1-338-18914-8

I Am Made of Shapes

by Liza Charlesworth

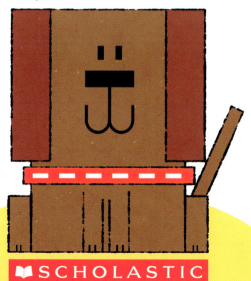

I Am Made of Shapes

by Liza Charlesworth

No part of this publication may be reproduced, stored in a retrieval system, or transmitted in any form or by any means, electronic, mechanical, photocopying, recording, or otherwise, without written permission of the publisher. For information regarding permission, write to Scholastic Inc., Attention: Permissions Department, 557 Broadway, New York, NY 10012.

ISBN: 978-1-338-18915-5
Illustrated by Steve Mack
Art Director: Tannaz Fassihi; Designer: Michelle H. Kim

Copyright © 2017 by Liza Charlesworth. All rights reserved. Published by Scholastic Inc.

10 9 68 21 22 23/0

Printed in China. First printing, June 2017.

Some Pumpkins

by Liza Charlesworth

www.scholastic.com

ISBN: 978-1-338-18915-5

Some Pumpkins

by Liza Charlesworth

No part of this publication may be reproduced, stored in a retrieval system, or transmitted in any form or by any means, electronic, mechanical, photocopying, recording, or otherwise, without written permission of the publisher. For information regarding permission, write to Scholastic Inc., Attention: Permissions Department, 557 Broadway, New York, NY 10012.

ISBN: 978-1-338-18916-2
Illustrated by Steve Mack
Art Director: Tannaz Fassihi; Designer: Michelle H. Kim

Copyright © 2017 by Liza Charlesworth. All rights reserved. Published by Scholastic Inc.

10 9   6 8   21 22 23/0

Printed in China. First printing, June 2017.

Rainbow Town

by Liza Charlesworth

ISBN: 978-1-338-18916-2

Rainbow Town

by Liza Charlesworth

No part of this publication may be reproduced, stored in a retrieval system, or transmitted in any form or by any means, electronic, mechanical, photocopying, recording, or otherwise, without written permission of the publisher. For information regarding permission, write to Scholastic Inc., Attention: Permissions Department, 557 Broadway, New York, NY 10012.

ISBN: 978-1-338-18917-9
Illustrated by Steve Mack
Art Director: Tannaz Fassihi; Designer: Michelle H. Kim

Copyright © 2017 by Liza Charlesworth. All rights reserved. Published by Scholastic Inc.

10 9   6 8   21 22 23/0

Printed in China. First printing, June 2017.

www.scholastic.com

ISBN: 978-1-338-18917-

EAN

Play Date

by Liza Charlesworth

Play Date

by Liza Charlesworth

No part of this publication may be reproduced, stored in a retrieval system, or transmitted in any form or by any means, electronic, mechanical, photocopying, recording, or otherwise, without written permission of the publisher. For information regarding permission, write to Scholastic Inc., Attention: Permissions Department, 557 Broadway, New York, NY 10012.

ISBN: 978-1-338-18918-6
Illustrated by Steve Mack
Art Director: Tannaz Fassihi; Designer: Michelle H. Kim

Copyright © 2017 by Liza Charlesworth. All rights reserved. Published by Scholastic Inc.

10 9   68   21 22 23/0

Printed in China. First printing, June 2017.

ISBN: 978-1-338-18918-6

www.scholastic.com

9 781338 189186

Super Mouse

by Liza Charlesworth

Super Mouse

by Liza Charlesworth

No part of this publication may be reproduced, stored in a retrieval system, or transmitted in any form or by any means, electronic, mechanical, photocopying, recording, or otherwise, without written permission of the publisher. For information regarding permission, write to Scholastic Inc., Attention: Permissions Department, 557 Broadway, New York, NY 10012.

ISBN: 978-1-338-18919-3
Illustrated by Steve Mack
Art Director: Tannaz Fassihi; Designer: Michelle H. Kim

Copyright © 2017 by Liza Charlesworth. All rights reserved. Published by Scholastic Inc.

10 9   68   21 22 23/0

Printed in China. First printing, June 2017.

www.scholastic.com

ISBN: 978-1-338-18919-3

You See

by Liza Charlesworth

SCHOLASTIC

You See

by Liza Charlesworth

No part of this publication may be reproduced, stored in a retrieval system, or transmitted in any form or by any means, electronic, mechanical, photocopying, recording, or otherwise, without written permission of the publisher. For information regarding permission, write to Scholastic Inc., Attention: Permissions Department, 557 Broadway, New York, NY 10012.

ISBN: 978-1-338-18920-9
Illustrated by Steve Mack
Art Director: Tannaz Fassihi; Designer: Michelle H. Kim

Copyright © 2017 by Liza Charlesworth. All rights reserved. Published by Scholastic Inc.

10 9   6 8   21 22 23/0

Printed in China. First printing, June 2017.

"You see an ice cream cone."

ISBN: 978-1-338-18920-9

My Pet Rock

by Liza Charlesworth

My Pet Rock

by Liza Charlesworth

No part of this publication may be reproduced, stored in a retrieval system, or transmitted in any form or by any means, electronic, mechanical, photocopying, recording, or otherwise, without written permission of the publisher. For information regarding permission, write to Scholastic Inc., Attention: Permissions Department, 557 Broadway, New York, NY 10012.

ISBN: 978-1-338-18921-6
Illustrated by Steve Mack
Art Director: Tannaz Fassihi; Designer: Michelle H. Kim

Copyright © 2017 by Liza Charlesworth. All rights reserved. Published by Scholastic Inc.

10 9   68   21 22 23/0

Printed in China. First printing, June 2017.

www.scholastic.com

ISBN: 978-1-338-18921-6

Best Friends

by Liza Charlesworth

Best Friends

by Liza Charlesworth

No part of this publication may be reproduced, stored in a retrieval system, or transmitted in any form or by any means, electronic, mechanical, photocopying, recording, or otherwise, without written permission of the publisher. For information regarding permission, write to Scholastic Inc., Attention: Permissions Department, 557 Broadway, New York, NY 10012.

ISBN: 978-1-338-18922-3
Illustrated by Kevin Zimmer
Art Director: Tannaz Fassihi; Designer: Michelle H. Kim

Copyright © 2017 by Liza Charlesworth. All rights reserved. Published by Scholastic Inc.

10 9   6 8   21 22 23/0

Printed in China. First printing, June 2017.

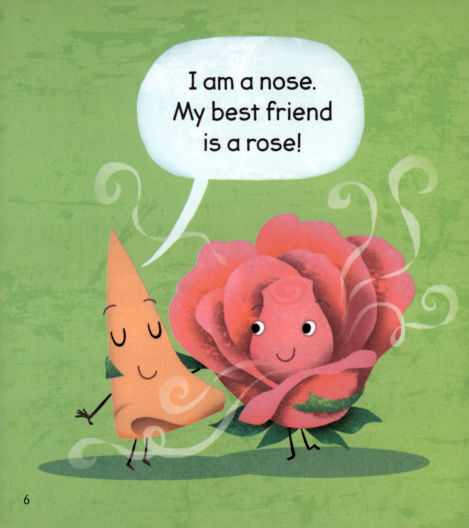

www.scholastic.com

ISBN: 978-1-338-18922-

EAN

The Best Color

by Liza Charlesworth

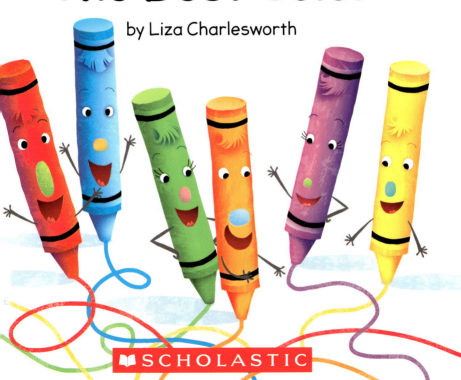

SCHOLASTIC

The Best Color

by Liza Charlesworth

No part of this publication may be reproduced, stored in a retrieval system, or transmitted in any form or by any means, electronic, mechanical, photocopying, recording, or otherwise, without written permission of the publisher. For information regarding permission, write to Scholastic Inc., Attention: Permissions Department, 557 Broadway, New York, NY 10012.

ISBN: 978-1-338-18923-0
Illustrated by Kevin Zimmer
Art Director: Tannaz Fassihi; Designer: Michelle H. Kim

Copyright © 2017 by Liza Charlesworth. All rights reserved. Published by Scholastic Inc.

10 9   68   21 22 23/0

Printed in China. First printing, June 2017.

ISBN: 978-1-338-18923-0

Pigs in Wigs

by Liza Charlesworth

Pigs in Wigs

by Liza Charlesworth

No part of this publication may be reproduced, stored in a retrieval system, or transmitted in any form or by any means, electronic, mechanical, photocopying, recording, or otherwise, without written permission of the publisher. For information regarding permission, write to Scholastic Inc., Attention: Permissions Department, 557 Broadway, New York, NY 10012.

ISBN: 978-1-338-18924-7
Illustrated by Kevin Zimmer
Art Director: Tannaz Fassihi; Designer: Michelle H. Kim

Copyright © 2017 by Liza Charlesworth. All rights reserved. Published by Scholastic Inc.

10 9 8 7 6 5 4 3 2 1   21 22 23/0

Printed in China. First printing, June 2017.

www.scholastic.com

ISBN: 978-1-338-18924-7

Eight Arms

by Liza Charlesworth

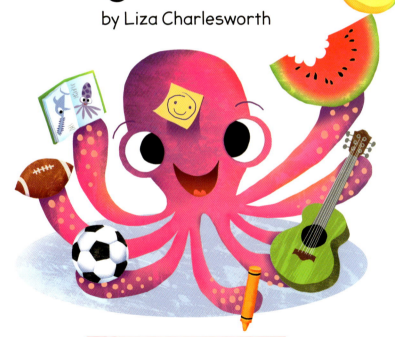

SCHOLASTIC

Eight Arms

by Liza Charlesworth

No part of this publication may be reproduced, stored in a retrieval system, or transmitted in any form or by any means, electronic, mechanical, photocopying, recording, or otherwise, without written permission of the publisher. For information regarding permission, write to Scholastic Inc., Attention: Permissions Department, 557 Broadway, New York, NY 10012.

ISBN: 978-1-338-18926-1
Illustrated by Kevin Zimmer
Art Director: Tannaz Fassihi; Designer: Michelle H. Kim

Copyright © 2017 by Liza Charlesworth. All rights reserved. Published by Scholastic Inc.

10 9   68   21 22 23/0

Printed in China. First printing, June 2017.

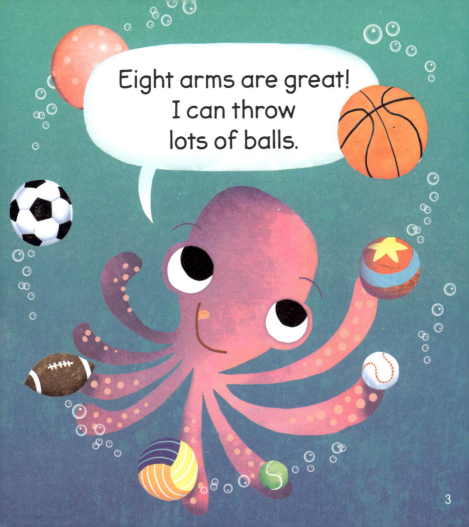

We Are Twins

by Liza Charlesworth

www.scholastic.com

ISBN: 978-1-338-18927-8

We Are Twins

by Liza Charlesworth

No part of this publication may be reproduced, stored in a retrieval system, or transmitted in any form or by any means, electronic, mechanical, photocopying, recording, or otherwise, without written permission of the publisher. For information regarding permission, write to Scholastic Inc., Attention: Permissions Department, 557 Broadway, New York, NY 10012.

ISBN: 978-1-338-18927-8
Illustrated by Kevin Zimmer
Art Director: Tannaz Fassihi; Designer: Michelle H. Kim

Copyright © 2017 by Liza Charlesworth. All rights reserved. Published by Scholastic Inc.

10 9   68   21 22 23/0

Printed in China. First printing, June 2017.

www.scholastic.com

ISBN: 978-1-338-18926-1

In the Rain

by Liza Charlesworth

In the Rain

by Liza Charlesworth

No part of this publication may be reproduced, stored in a retrieval system, or transmitted in any form or by any means, electronic, mechanical, photocopying, recording, or otherwise, without written permission of the publisher. For information regarding permission, write to Scholastic Inc., Attention: Permissions Department, 557 Broadway, New York, NY 10012.

ISBN: 978-1-338-18928-5
Illustrated by Kevin Zimmer
Art Director: Tannaz Fassihi; Designer: Michelle H. Kim

Copyright © 2017 by Liza Charlesworth. All rights reserved. Published by Scholastic Inc.

10 9   68   21 22 23/0

Printed in China. First printing, June 2017.

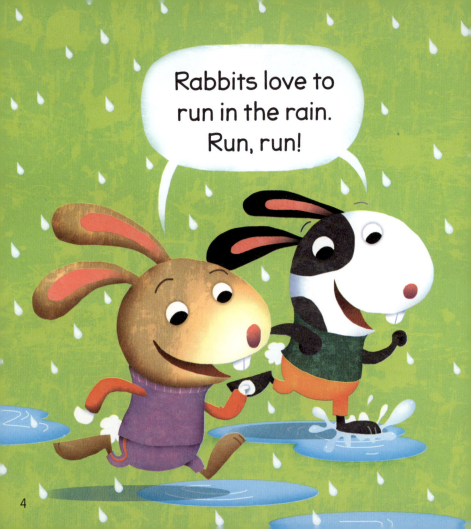

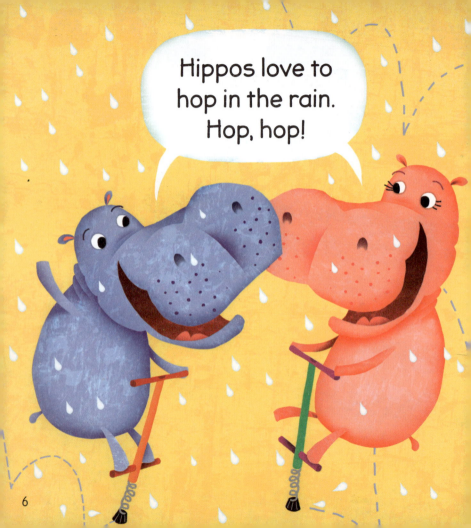

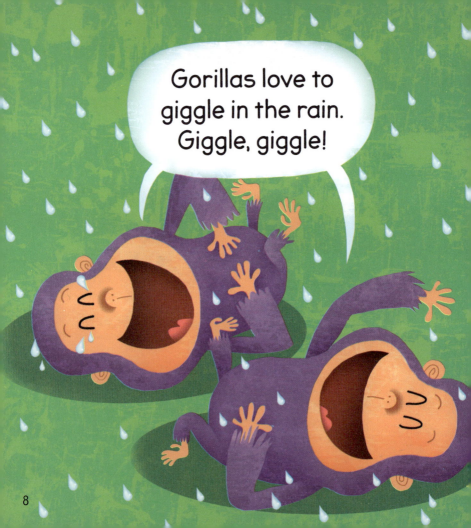

www.scholastic.com

ISBN: 978-1-338-18928-5

Cool School

by Liza Charlesworth

Cool School

by Liza Charlesworth

No part of this publication may be reproduced, stored in a retrieval system, or transmitted in any form or by any means, electronic, mechanical, photocopying, recording, or otherwise, without written permission of the publisher. For information regarding permission, write to Scholastic Inc., Attention: Permissions Department, 557 Broadway, New York, NY 10012.

ISBN: 978-1-338-18929-2
Illustrated by Kevin Zimmer
Art Director: Tannaz Fassihi; Designer: Michelle H. Kim

Copyright © 2017 by Liza Charlesworth. All rights reserved. Published by Scholastic Inc.

10 9 68 21 22 23/0

Printed in China. First printing, June 2017.

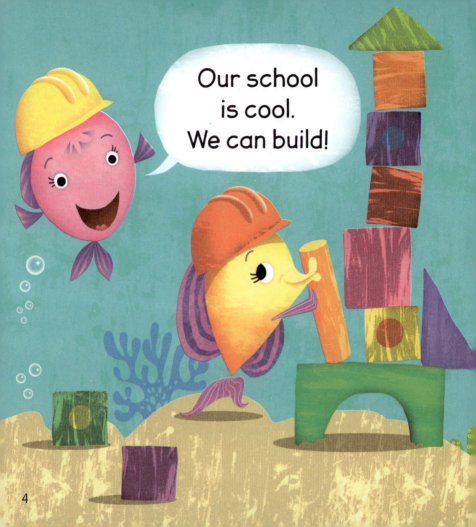

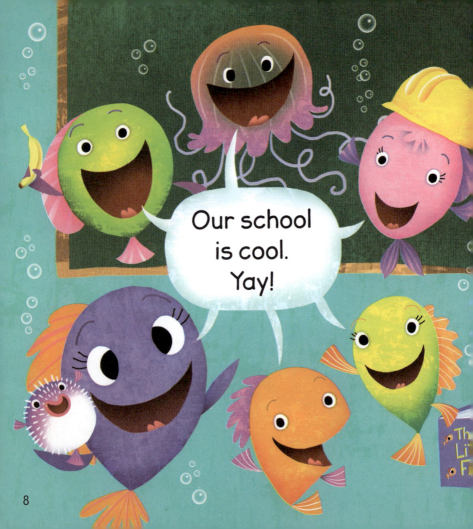

Kiss This Frog

by Liza Charlesworth

SCHOLASTIC

www.scholastic.com

ISBN: 978-1-338-18929-2

Kiss This Frog

by Liza Charlesworth

No part of this publication may be reproduced, stored in a retrieval system, or transmitted in any form or by any means, electronic, mechanical, photocopying, recording, or otherwise, without written permission of the publisher. For information regarding permission, write to Scholastic Inc., Attention: Permissions Department, 557 Broadway, New York, NY 10012.

ISBN: 978-1-338-18930-8
Illustrated by Kevin Zimmer
Art Director: Tannaz Fassihi; Designer: Michelle H. Kim

Copyright © 2017 by Liza Charlesworth. All rights reserved. Published by Scholastic Inc.

10 9   68   21 22 23/0

Printed in China. First printing, June 2017.

www.scholastic.com

ISBN: 978-1-338-18930-8

I See a Robot

by Liza Charlesworth

I See a Robot

by Liza Charlesworth

No part of this publication may be reproduced, stored in a retrieval system, or transmitted in any form or by any means, electronic, mechanical, photocopying, recording, or otherwise, without written permission of the publisher. For information regarding permission, write to Scholastic Inc., Attention: Permissions Department, 557 Broadway, New York, NY 10012.

ISBN: 978-1-338-18931-5
Illustrated by Kevin Zimmer
Art Director: Tannaz Fassihi; Designer: Michelle H. Kim

Copyright © 2017 by Liza Charlesworth. All rights reserved. Published by Scholastic Inc.

10 9   68   21 22 23/0

Printed in China. First printing, June 2017.

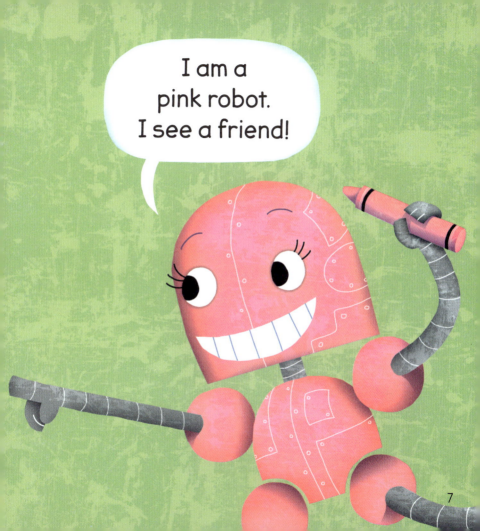

I Will Not Eat the Cake

by Liza Charlesworth

www.scholastic.com

ISBN: 978-1-338-18931-5

I Will Not Eat the Cake

by Liza Charlesworth

No part of this publication may be reproduced, stored in a retrieval system, or transmitted in any form or by any means, electronic, mechanical, photocopying, recording, or otherwise, without written permission of the publisher. For information regarding permission, write to Scholastic Inc., Attention: Permissions Department, 557 Broadway, New York, NY 10012.

ISBN: 978-1-338-18932-2
Illustrated by Kevin Zimmer
Art Director: Tannaz Fassihi; Designer: Michelle H. Kim

Copyright © 2017 by Liza Charlesworth. All rights reserved. Published by Scholastic Inc.

10 9 68 21 22 23/0

Printed in China. First printing, June 2017.

ISBN: 978-1-338-18932-2

www.scholastic.com

WAR AI

A WILD POEM WITH WEIRD PICTURES

Dedicated to Miss Erin Ruth McKillen

*Go gcúití an Tiarna do shaothar leat, agus go
dtuga an Tiarna Dia Iosrael luach
saothair iomlán duit ós rud é gur tháinig tú
ag lorg dídine faoi scáth a sciathán.*

The LORD recompense thy work,
and a full reward be given thee
of the LORD God of Israel,
under whose wings thou art come to trust.
Ruth 2.12

DAVID Z CROOKES

All rights reserved. No part of this publication may be reproduced, stored in a retrieval system or transmitted, in any form or by any means, electronic, mechanical, photocopying, recording or otherwise, without the prior permission of the author.

Printed in 2022 by Shanway Press,
15 Crumlin Road, Belfast BT14 6AA

ISBN: 978-1-910044-41-4

© 2022 David Z Crookes

FOREWORD

I should confess that 'War and Peace' was written in order to provide the Renaissance song 'Watkin's Ale' with a decorous text. The poem has already appeared in *FoMRHI Quarterly* 121 (May, 2012), whose genial editor, Mr Christopher Goodwin, does not object to its new manifestation. You won't understand the rhythm of the poem unless you look up the tune of 'Watkin's Ale' on the internet.

'War and Peace' has a perceptible all-Ireland dimension. Bray town centre appears on the front cover. Offaly, Belfast, and Cork feature in three of the pictures. ('Old Friends' is based on a medieval icon of Naboth.) For its part the rear cover involves a severely stylised view of the Blue Lough, near Annalong, Co. Down, where the author sometimes goes for a swim, and where Snow White is believed to have conferred with Arthur O'Shaughnessy. History can be a jolly complicated business.

DZC

An anti-postcolonial boy
Demobilized the troops in Troy;
He paved a path for Toby Belch,
And braved the wrath of Mr Quelch.
  His name was Peregrine:
  He claimed that kerosene
  Made his young terrapin
    Rather caustic!
  Though he loved carpentry,
  When he drank Chardonnay,
  He found it hard to say
    'Vladivostok'.
If the legend is true,
He invented the letter Q;
What we do know for sure
Is that Peregrine sold manure.

Mr Quelch

It fell upon a summer's day
That Peregrine arrived in Bray;
He called at seven nursing-homes,
And lifted all their garden gnomes.
    Flushed with his robbery,
    He drove to Offaly,
    Where he unlawfully
        Cooked a peacock;
    Finding a cedar-tree,
    Peregrine eagerly
    Started to read from the
        Book of Enoch.
Then he lit his cigar,
And adjourned to the Dungeon Bar;
He took care not to say
That he worked for the CIA.

Offaly

While Peregrine was drinking stout,
The garden gnomes were breaking out;
They overturned their captor's van,
And said, 'We need a battle-plan.
    We are not ornaments,
    We should buy armaments;
    We can make parliaments
        Gyre and gimble;
    Gnomes will rule Bangalore,
    Belfast and Elsinore:
    We shall have vengeance for
        Lambert Simnel!
Gnomic might must prevail:
Human culture is bound to fail.
Death to both king and queen,
Death to ladies who sing JOLENE.'

Overturned

The gnomes encouraged German banks
To help them purchase Sherman tanks.
They thought that they would lose the war
Unless they used the armoured car;
    They felt that Saracens
    Suited their garrisons:
    They found Polaris com-
        Pletely useless!
    They looked up Clausewitz,
    Drew maps of Austerlitz,
    Read E M Forster and
        P G Wodehouse.
They would launch their crusade
With a sortie against Belgrade;
Once the Danube was won,
Europeans would cut and run.

The Writers' Cafe in Linenhall Library where the gnomes looked up Clausewitz, and a lot of the author's work is done on weekdays

While Serbia fought with might and main,
The rest of Europe went insane;
Dictators warned of 'gnomes within',
By which they meant one's kith and kin.
    Short men were pointed at,
    Rounded up, pounced upon --
    Old friends denounced them as
        Dwarfish hybrids;
    Neo-McCarthyites
    Went round with Armalites,
    Gunning down farmers with
        Elvish eyelids.
Uniformed teenage brats
Murdered men who wore pixie hats;
Overweight musketeers
Slaughtered boys who had pointed ears.

Old Friends

Both judge and jury lost their jobs
As rules were made by ruthless mobs;
Survivors still recall the time
When ev'rything became a crime.
   People were butchered for
   Using computers, or
   Riding on scooters, or
      Quoting Milton;
   One poor transgressor was
   Shot for possession of
   Handwritten essays by
      Paris Hilton.
If a boy stole a peach,
He was hung from a copper beech;
If a girl smiled in church,
She was hung from a silver birch.

The Writer of Essays

Well, gnomes (like cars and caravans)
Are made by human artisans,
But now that gnomes were driving tanks,
It seemed insane to swell their ranks.
    Former gnome-factories
    Turned out phylacteries,
    Trampolines, tractors, and
        Treble viols;
    Owners of garden stores
    Said to their paramours,
    'War kills the market for
        Rebel icons.'
When the gnomes heard, they cried,
'We are threatened with ethnicide;
How can we reproduce?
All our thinking has been obtuse.'

Treble Viols

Four gnomes approached the Cork police,
And said, 'We want to sue for peace.'
The CIA got Peregrine
To set up talks in West Berlin.
    Snow White persuaded the
    Gnomes that invading the
    Homes of Belgrade was a
        Lethal folly;
    Arthur O'Shaughnessy's
    Artful diplomacy
    Led men and gnomes to seek
        Peace with honour.
Peregrine sold his van,
Now a sadder and wiser man.
Songs are not what they seem:
Mine is merely a fading dream.

A fading dream of Cork police station

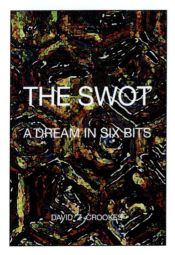
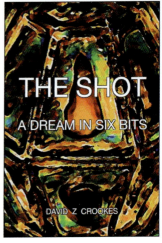
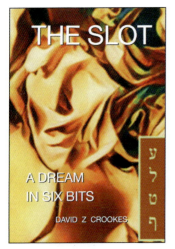

WAR AND PEACE
follows DZC's
brilliant trilogy
THE SHOT,
THE SWOT and
THE SLOT
which are all also
available from
Shanway Press.
All three are poems of
72 verses.